ITS OKAY TO SAY OUCH

Created By:

NAOMIE BANATTE

Illustrations By:

FUUJI TAKASHI

In loving memory of
Naisha B. and Ms. Rita Owens

In honor of:
Safe People across the world who
live to make a difference in the lives
of our youth.

I was sad when I woke up for school today. Today is another day that the bad monster might hurt me. Today is another day that I would feel pain. Today is just another day I would whisper to myself "Ouch it hurts".

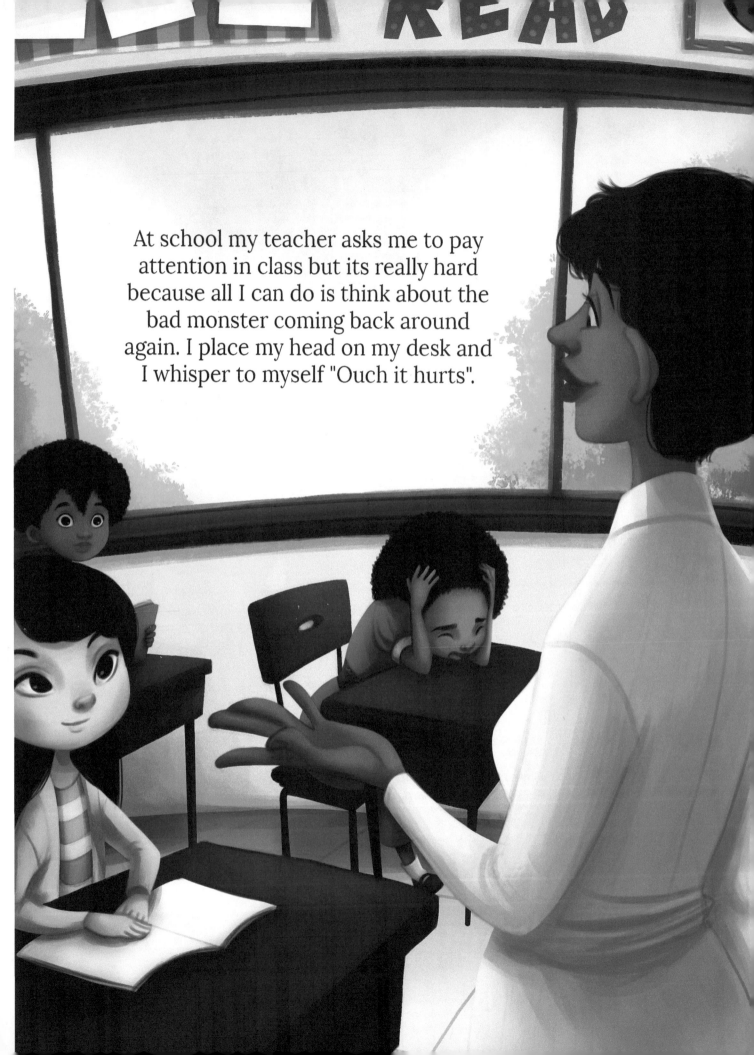

At school my teacher asks me to pay attention in class but its really hard because all I can do is think about the bad monster coming back around again. I place my head on my desk and I whisper to myself "Ouch it hurts".

Recess is the best part of my
day because I can be all alone.
I really don't want to play.

I rather look for a spot on the
playground where I can sit all
by myself .

I much rather quietly watch
the other kids play.

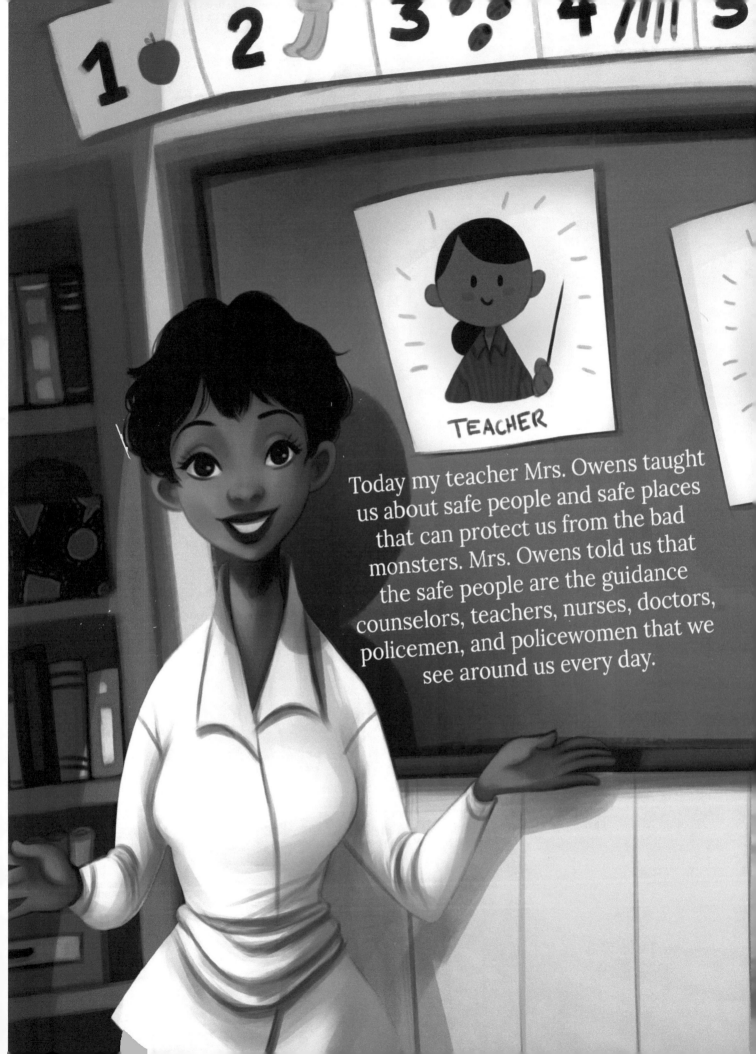

Today my teacher Mrs. Owens taught us about safe people and safe places that can protect us from the bad monsters. Mrs. Owens told us that the safe people are the guidance counselors, teachers, nurses, doctors, policemen, and policewomen that we see around us every day.

The safe people have force fields said Mrs. Owens and if we told them what the bad monsters did to harm us, they would give us our very own special force field. The force fields will keep the bad monsters away from us and protect us from harm.

Sometimes the bad monster hurts my body. Sometimes the bad monster hurts my feelings. Sometimes the bad monster hurts both my body and my feelings and it makes me so so sad. The monster told me not to tell anyone because if I did, it would harm me even more so I place my head on my desk and just whisper to myself "Ouch it hurts."

I thought about what Mrs. Owens said and I wondered if I could get enough courage to tell the safe people about the bad monster. I wanted one of those special force fields so badly.

See, the thing is that I knew that I didn't misbehave and I was great at following all of the rules so I couldn't understand why the monster would want to hurt me. I didn't do anything wrong to the monster or anyone else. I really want the bad monster to stop.

After school while Mrs. Owens was all alone in our classroom.
I walked up to her desk and began whispering "Ouch".

It was really hard to say aloud so I whispered once, "ouch it hurts", then
I whispered again a little louder this time "ouch it hurts" but Mrs.
Owens asked me to repeat myself since she couldn't hear my whispers.

I took a deep breath and said as loud as I could, "OUCH IT HURTS". What hurts?! Said Mrs. Owens. I then told her all about the bad monster and even showed her some of the ways that the monster has been hurting me.

Mrs. Owens gave me a huge hug and told me that it was Okay to say OUCH. She also told me that she thinks that I am very special and very brave. Then she quickly called the other safe people and they began building a brand new force field just for me.

Before I knew it, the force field had been built and the monster wasn't allowed to come anywhere near me ever again.

The bad monster could no longer
harm me and I was finally safe.

Wow! That was pretty easy. I wish I told the safe people about the bad monster alot sooner. Telling a safe person wasn't as scary as I thought.

Today, I woke up and got ready for school but this time I was excited because I no longer had to worry about the bad monster, it was far far away. The sun was shining and I was in my cool force field.

I can pay attention in class and it's so fun to play with my friends again. I feel great because I was brave, and because I decided to be brave, I am now safe.

I am so glad that I have safe people around me because I now know that it "It's Okay to Say OUCH". Please don't ever be afraid to say "OUCH". You can have your very own force field if you need one. You are brave and special too!

About Author

According to https://www.Childhelp.org, "Every year more than 3.6million referrals are made to child protection agencies involving more than 6.6million children (a referral can include multiple children). The United States has one of the worst records among industrialized nations –losing on average between four and seven children every day to child abuse and neglect. A report of child abuse is made every 10 seconds".

Research has found that successful child abuse interventions both reduce risk factors and promote protective factors to ensure the well-being of children and families. In addition, protective factors create conditions in families and communities that, when present, increase the health and well-being of children and families both mentally and physically allowing for a greater life expectancy than those who experience multiple occurrences of abuse.

My name is Naomie Banatte. I am the Author of; "It's Okay to Say OUCH". I wrote this inspirational reading in order to bring awareness to the child abuse and domestic violence epidemic across the globe. My passion for helping children inspired me to create a comfortable and Kid- friendly space where we all can address some of the issues regarding this silent epidemic with our youth.

This contemporary realistic fiction book is near and dear to my heart because I too have been a victim of child abuse as an adolescent. Although I was fortunate to have had a very supportive and loving community, the adverse effects of the trauma that I have experienced followed me into adulthood. Today, not only am I survivor, I am more than a resilient conqueror. I currently have an Associates Degree in Early Childhood Education and a Bachelors Degree in Human Learning Development with a concentration in Child Development and Counseling. My three handsome, loving, funny, active, and intelligent sons are the center of my world. I could not have achieved so much without their love and support.

My ultimate mission is to contribute to the preventative efforts and to help the abused children of this world understand that they can be more than conquerors as well. Please join me in this mission to end child abuse for all of our beautiful children. After all, they are our future and our future should know that "It's Okay to Say OUCH".

References
Childhelp A Non-Profit Charity Aiding Victims of Child Abuse http://w-
ww.childhelp.org

Anon, (2018). Child Abuse and Neglect: Mandated Reporting Require-
ments for Employees, Volunteers, and Contractors of Georgia Public
Schools. [online] Available at: https://www.prosolutionstraining.com/
[Accessed 20 Jun. 2018].

Printed in the United States of America

First Printing 2018

COUNSELOR

DOCTOR

NURSE

POLICE

TEAC

CPSIA information can be obtained
at www.ICGtesting.com
Printed in the USA
BVHW020309160320
574931BV00002B/3